*Old warehouses and bridge over the Teifi at Cardigan*

# THE CEREDIGION
# COAST PATH

## Mike Salter

FOLLY PUBLICATIONS

*View northwards towards Pendinaslochdyn*

## ACKNOWLEDGEMENTS

The photographs are all by Mike Salter, who also drew the maps. Thanks to the staff at Aspect Design for their help in preparing illustrations and generally assembling the artwork of the book ready for publication.

## DISCLAIMER

Every effort has been made to ensure information in this book is accurate and up-to-date, but the author/publisher does not accept any responsibility for any accidents to users, nor is any responsibility accepted for any problems that might arise through any of the information given being inaccurate, incomplete or out-of-date. Please take careful note of the suggestions about outdoor safety given on page 7.

## AUTHOR'S NOTES

Distances are given in miles, still the most familiar unit of measurement for most British people. Although modern Ordnance Survey maps are metric, heights and amounts of climb in this book are given in feet, mainly so as to avoid any ambiguity as to whether an m folowing a figure means miles or metres. The contours on the Landranger maps are at 10 metre intervals, i.e. crossing three of them means roughly 100 feet of climb.

## ABOUT THE AUTHOR

Mike Salter is 53 and has been a professional author and publisher since 1988. He is particularly interested in the planning and layout of medieval buildings and has a huge collection of plans of castles and old churches he has measured during tours (mostly by bicycle and motorcycle) throughout all parts of the British Isles since 1968. Wolverhampton born and bred, Mike now lives in an old cottage beside the Malvern Hills. Since walking Land's End to John O'Groats in 2004 following his 50th birthday he has done many other long distance backpacking trails. He is a life member of both the YHA and English Heritage, and he is also a member of the Backpackers Club and the Mountain Bothies Association. His other interests include railways, board games, morris dancing and calling folk dances and playing percussion with an occasional ceilidh band.

*Ynys-Lochtyn*

## CONTENTS

# INTRODUCTION

The Ceredigion Coast Path runs from the Teifi estuary at Cardigan and runs to Ynyslas on the south side of the Dovey estuary. Starting at Cardigan works best since the sun and prevailing wind will mostly be behind you. Ynyslas has a good bus service to Aberystwyth but does not make a very exciting ending for the walk, so this book describes a delightful extension to Machynlleth.This gives an ending at a place with a rail connection and more things of interest to see, and also allows a connection onto the Owain Glyndwr Way, which is used for the last mile into the town. Cardigan has no rail service but is connected by hourly buses to Fishguard, which has two trains a day connecting with ferries to Rosslare in Eire, one in the early hours of the morning and the other in the afternoon. Buses also run through to and from the station at Haverfordwest, which has trains at about two hourly intervals from Swansea and places further east, some through trains coming down from Manchester via Shrewsbury and Hereford. The A487 running parallel to the walk also has hourly buses for much of the day between Cardigan and Aberystwyth.

Between New Quay and Borth a system of paths following the coast within about 300 yards of the shore is well established. Between Cardigan and Cwmtyd (near New Quay) there are five sections of the coast each up to three miles long where formerly no public paths or roads existed. In order to make a route from Cardigan to Ynyslas the county council is trying to create a number of new sections of path by purchasing strips of land from landowners under compulsory orders. The scheme is controversial and has been resisted by some landowners, especially along one section between Gwbert and Mwnt which would cut across a farm park which is a tourist attraction where an admission fee is payable. This section remains incomplete and is still subject to review. The alternative inland route given here through Y Ferwig is, however, pleasant enough and does not by-pass anything on the coast of much architectural, historical or geological interest, but the nature reserve of Cardigan Island is only viewed from a considerable distance. Gwbert is essentially an hotel, golf and caravan site complex of no great beauty and only reachable from Cardigan by walking on (or close to) a main road, so excluding it from your walk is no great hardship. Further north a two mile section of coast west of Aberporth will in any case remain out of bounds to walkers because it contains an RAF base and firing range.

Overall the walk is quite strenuous, with many steep climbs of up to three to four hundred feet, some of them involving long flights of steps. There is not much boggy ground, except on the extra extension section beside the Dovey estuary but you will need proper boots and also gaiters, since there will be fields to cross where there is no marked path and the grass may be long and wet in the summer. The new southern sections of the path are not well established as yet and the lengths of route between the newly installed bridges and gates are likely to be somewhat overgrown. There are numerous stiles and quite a lot of kissing gates and the older ones in particular tend to not allow enough space for people carrying backpacks.

Since the overall length of the route is not fully open yet many of the intended sign-boards have yet to be erected and there are no boards marking any official start or finish. North of New Quay the paths are fairly well signed, although only a few of the signs are the new ones specifically marking a path or road as being part of the coast path route.

*Wooden dolphin at Aberporth*

*View looking south back towards New Quay*

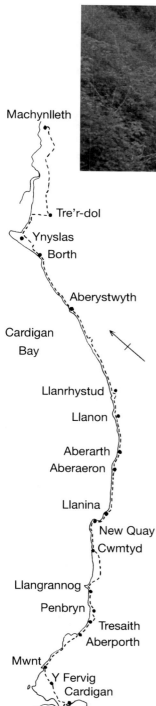

Machynlleth
Tre'r-dol
Ynyslas
Borth
Aberystwyth
Cardigan
Bay
Llanrhystud
Llanon
Aberarth
Aberaeron
Llanina
New Quay
Cwmtyd
Llangrannog
Penbryn
Tresaith
Aberporth
Mwnt
Y Fervig
Cardigan

The coastal resorts are very geared to the needs of holiday-makers and B&Bs are plentiful. There is a youth hostel at Poppit Sands four miles beyond Cardigan near the end of the Pembrokeshire Coast Path and another hostel at Borth, but there are no other hostels between them except for an independant hostel in Aberystwyth. Camp sites are numerous although most of them mainly cater for caravans and hardly any offer tent pitches giving shelter against strong winds coming in from the southwest, west, or north-west. There are many places where you can camp out wild near the shore without any facilities, although it isn't encouraged by the authorities or the farmers and is against bylaws in several places, particularly on National Trust lands and beside county council car-parks. It is unlikely you'll be arrested for camping, unless you are causing damage, noise or pollution, but you could be moved on. It is legal to stop for rest or refreshment whilst walking along a right-of-way but there is no right to erect any sort of shelter, however temporary. The basic rules about wild camping are to be discreet at all times and to leave no trace that you've been there. Use a tent with a flysheet of a colour that blends with the surroundings, pitch fairly late and leave early. Don't stay more than one night, or camp in large groups, light fires, leave rubbish or make noise, and don't pitch within sight of any road, farm or house unless you've obtained prior permission from the landowner.

There are plenty of public toilets along the Ceredigion coast and almost all of them have proper taps and washbasins rather than wall-units, In May those away from towns were open late (or all night), and in any case some have external drinking water taps. Most of the streams you will be crossing will have flowed over fields where animals graze so it isn't safe to drink water from them unless it has been boiled or made safe with tablets.

One or two short sections of the route are permissive paths rather than rights of way and thus could be closed, even if only for short periods, to allow agricultural or sporting activities or birds to nest. There are also a few sections of path which may be submerged by high tides. Usually there's a road alternative, but this may not be clearly signed and will add some mileage.

# ENVIRONMENTAL IMPACT

Basically: Leave nothing but footprints, take nothing but photographs & memories. So:
Don't leave any litter, even biodegradable material such as fruit cores and skins.
Don't pick flowers or damage trees and plants, except where necessary to clear a path.
Don't make lots unecessary noise, especially when passing through farmyards.
Don't get so close to animals that they become stressed and abandon their young.
Don't stray from the path on sections where you can clearly see its intended route.
Don't touch farming or forestry equipment, crops, timber stacks or building materials.
Leave all gates as you find them, whether open or closed.
Be discreet if wild camping (see page 5), and guard against all risk of starting fires.

Use public toilets where possible. If you have to go outdoors make sure you are at least 30m from running water and bury excrement in a small hole where it will decompose quicker. Do not bury tampons or sanitary towels. You will have to carry these out. Ideally you should also do this with toilet paper also, since it doesn't decompose quickly and will blow around if dug up by animals.

If you are taking a dog with you it will need to be on a short lead at all times since there are many sections where there are sheep, cows or breeding grounds for wild birds. Also you will need to think carefully about where you will be able to stay. Dogs are specifically banned from some of the beaches during the summer months and there are sections of permissive path where there are restrictions on dogs.

# NAVIGATIONAL AIDS

The route described in this book crosses the Ordnance Survey Landranger maps numbers 145, 146, and 135. You should carry a compass and know how to use it together with the map but its unlikely that you'll need to do this anywhere along this route, as there aren't long sections of bare moorland where you can get very lost.

*One of the newly erected coastal path signposts*

A useful item is a Global Positioning System. You can check your speed and distance, and time travelled, but best of all it will give you a grid reference accurate to a few feet. Those who like treasure hunting can additionally use the unit to find geocaches (website details given on page 20), of which there are many along the route. GPS units use up batteries quickly, and need a clear view of the sky, so they are not so good in woodland.

*Castell Bach fort, near Cwmtyd*

*Aberporth*

## OUTDOOR SAFETY

Careful walking and footwear that gives a reasonable grip is needed on some sections of the route. There are several lengths of path with unfenced sheer drops, although these are mostly fairly short and usually you can walk several feet away from the actual edge. Children, will, however, need a lot of close supervision.

Sort out any problems with feet, footwear or socks immediately. Make sure you carry enough dry clothes to remain warm even in the most wet and stormy conditions, and carry enough food and drink so that you don't have to rush unduly or take risks. Take care not to be cut-off by the tide on beaches. If in doubt stay above high-tide level. Be realistic when estimating distances. Cliff-top paths meandering around headlands and inlets go further than they look on the map. Don't expect to make more than three miles an hour even if fit, lightly loaded and weather conditions are favourable. Averaging two miles an hour will be good going for people carrying camping equipment on steeply graded paths.

*The Parliament House at Machynlleth*

# ROUTE DESCRIPTION

## CARDIGAN - ABERPORTH

Cardigan (or Aberteifi - Mouth of the Teifi) was once the county town, although it is no longer an administrative centre and law courts are held in Lampeter and Aberystwyth. Cardigan has a reasonable range of shops and services. Warehouses and a Customs House (now offices) are reminders of the town's former importance as a port before the river silted up. Many of the High Street buildings are Victorian and there is a guildhall of 1858 over a covered market. The tourist information office lies in Bath House Road, off the west side of Pendre at the north end of the High Street.

Immediately north of the bridge over the river is the shored-up wall of the castle. It seems to have been established here in 1171 by Lord Rhys ap Gruffydd to replace an earlier ringwork further west. Here at Christmas 1176 he staged the earliest recorded eisteddfod, with separate competitions for poetry and pipers and other musicians. The castle was sold in 1200 to King John and was captured by the Welsh in 1215 and 1231, and also by William Marshal the Younger in 1223. The remains probably date from a rebuilding by the Marshals in the 1240s, and the town was walled in by the next owner, Robert Waleran. Two U-shaped towers face SE, and embedded in the later house is what appears to be the westernmost of a pair of towers of a gatehouse of c1280-1300. The defences were dismantled after the castle was stormed by Parliamentary troops in 1644.

To the east of the castle, in a graveyard between St Mary's Street and the shore, is the parish church with a 14th century chancel with fragments of old glass in the 15th century east window. The spacious nave was partly rebuilt in 1702-3, and shortly afterwards the 16th century west tower collapsed and required rebuilding. There is a house on the site of the Benedicture priory which adjoined the church. It was home of the poet Katherine Fowler in the 1630s after her marriage to James Phillipps, and was remodelled by John Nash in the 1790s for Thomas Johns of Hafod. In William St is the fine Bethania Chapel of 1848 with a Doric portico and other classical features. The ruins of the Premonstratensian Abbey of St Dogmaels lie only just over a mile west of the town.

To start the walk from Cardigan castle and bridge go west down Quay St, passing a supermarket with public toilets opposite on the right hand side. At the car park on the shore climb up slightly to cross over an edge of Netpool Park and go down a road. When it ends at a locked gate a path goes between the fencing and the shoreline, which is wooded, so there are only occasional glimpses of the Teifi estuary. Go over a wobbly stile on the right to walk along the western edge of a ploughed field to Old Castle farm, 1m from Cardigan. Hidden under vegetation and not visible from the route is a ringwork which is probably the site of the original castle of Aberteifi built in 1093 by Roger de Montgomery. It was rebuilt by the de Clares in 1110 and 1159, and survived a Welsh attack in 1136, but was destroyed by Rhys ap Gruffydd in 1165 and later replaced by the castle at Cardigan.

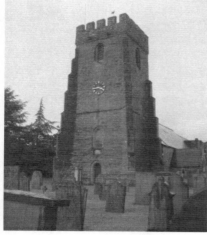

*St Mary's Church, Cardigan*

*Wall and tower of Cardigan Castle*

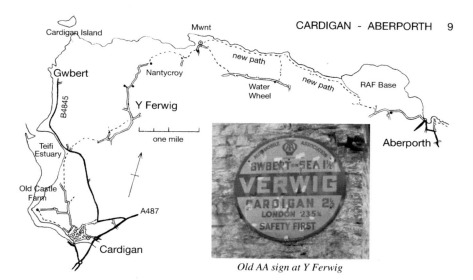

*Old AA sign at Y Ferwig*

Climb up the road eastwards from Old Castle Farm and turn left at a T-junction. Ignore the path going off right where there is a seat at the start of a double bend, but take another path forking off right further down when the road again bends left. Pass through several kissing gates (all but the first now having their gates lying loose since they are too narrow to use otherwise) as you cross several fields and go through a short woodland section by the shore before arriving at B4548. Eventually the coast path may head north from here but for now go right just a few yards, then left up a driveway (not signed). Beyond the house a pleasant track climbs up in a NE direction to give a view of Cardigan and go through the edge of a wood. Turn left onto a drive of a house and at a junction go left to climb up to where a path goes off right through Bryn-Pedr farmyard. Pass several fields (and a seat) to turn left onto a road heading NW through Y Ferwig, 4m from Cardigan. The village has no shop and the only item of interest is an old AA sign on a building giving the English spelling of the name (Verwig) and several distances, including that from London.

Keep right at the junction at the end of Y Ferwig and follow the zig-zagging road past two farms to a third farm at Nantycroy. The camping field here offers shelter against a westerly wind. A bridleway continues through the yard as a muddy track and then goes across fields to Clos y Graig. Bend left to go through gorse bushes without reaching the farm road, and the path brings you down to Mwnt, 6m from Cardigan. There are toilets and information boards, a sandy beach, and a kiln for burning lime back in the days when lime was spread on fields to make the grass grow better on poor soils. There is also a camp site, but the field is very exposed. Just below the headland (National Trust land) is the small whitewashed church of Holy Cross. The small single chamber is probably 13th or 14th century, although the passage and steps on the north side to give access to a loft over a former screen are 15th century. and the font is Norman.

The next three miles fairly closely following the coastline has fine new bridges and gates and stiles but the very newly established path is steep in places and has yet to be much walked. It may be overgrown without much of a marked path in some parts and there's some wire across it in one place. The last section is a bulldozed track and this leads to a section, also partly newly cut, which goes inland high above the stream running down to Carreg Wynt. Two new signs direct you into an overgrown woodland path and then there's a difficult junction (obstructions of wire and fallen trees) to reach an older established path at SN 240515. Turn left to cross fields to the south of the military base. Just south of the hangars turn right down a track and turn left onto a road. Another left turn by some toilets brings you down a steep road to the western edge of Aberporth, 11m from Cardigan. The National Trust owns a waterwheel (currently much overgrown) at Llwnysgaw (SN 219515). To pass by this site use the bridleway leading SE up from the campsite at Mwnt, and walk east along the lane. A new path leading north through woods and then across fields just east of the waterwheel allows access back onto the new coastpath.

ABERPORTH is very much a holiday resort with good sandy beaches and several campsites. Here farmers from Llechryd beside the Teifi used to hold an annual feast on the beach between the hay and corn harvests. Follow the road round the first of two small bays to reach a corner of B4333. A path goes round the second bay and rises up just north of a set of toilets. Alternatively stay on B4333 a short distance and turn left at the crossroads to arrive at the same place past food and hardware shops and a pharmacy. There are also several hotels and pubs. The coast path is reached down a lane heading east just south of the end of the road and goes past the Coach House, a residence made from a converted and extended old railway carriage. Several more are passed over the next three hundred yards and there's another by a bend of the lane at Llangrannog. The coast path only goes as far as Tresaith, a small resort with a pub and beach-shop just over 12m from Cardigan. A new two mile long section of coast path is under construction but the approach to it will be very steep and it is no real hardship to follow the quiet, winding and partly wooded lanes slightly inland as there are several things to see here.

Climb up from the shore at Tresaith on a steep lane, noting the fine mural of a sailing ship on the gable end of the Ship Inn. When the road bends right at a bus stop go left and after four hundred yards left again on a road which bends to the left as it climbs steeply. Go left at a crossroads and before going left again at a T-junction glimpse (with difficulty) over the high bank the ancient pillar stone in the field. It is carved with the inscription Corbalengi Iacit Ordovs. Half a mile further on the church of St Michael at Penbryn appears on the left. The Norman nave of the church retains two tiny original north windows. The south wall is mostly 15th century, when the 13th century chancel was widened slightly to the north. The west porch is 17th century. Carry on down past the church and turn left to reach a National Trust estate where there is a cafe and toilets. Take the track on the right by the farm buildings just beyond and when the path divides go left to climb back up onto the cliff-tops. Another mile and a half brings you down into Llangrannog, 16m from Cardigan. There is a shop, pub, cafe and public toilets.

*Mural on Ship Inn, Tresaith*

*Distant view of Penbryn Church*

*Old railway carriage converted into a house at Llangrannog*

The next section of path is on National Trust land and climbs up from the shingle top of the beach at Llangrannog. Off the edge of the headland here is the island of Ynys Lochtyn. The path goes below the summit of the headland on which was the fort of Pendinaslochdyn, although there's not much in the way of ramparts and ditches to see. Half a mile east of here the path swings inland to pass the Urdd Centre, where youths are offered a fine range of outdoor and indoor pursuits. When the three mile section of clifftop path from here to Cwmtu is completed the inland route described below can be regarded as an attractive alternative to a very exposed clifftop path in wet and windy weather.

Follow the road through the centre down to turn left on B4321. After 250 yards fork left onto a minor road and then after half a mile take a path down through woods on the right. Cross over another path and reach B4321, only to immediately take a path on the left. It goes through woods, across a field, through a gate slightly to the right and then crosses another field to arrive just below an outbuilding of a house. Ignoring a second path going off on the right between two hedgerows at the same place, turn right up the drive of the house and turn left onto a lane which bends right after 400 yards. Go left at a sort of crossroads and left again soon afterwards. When the lane turns sharply left after 450 yards drop down right on a path. After three stiles/gates the path goes left to hug the contour with delightful views above the wooded ravine of a stream. Turn left onto a wider path coming up from the bottom and go left at a crossing of tracks in forestry to reach a lane and turn right. After crossing Afon Ffynnon Dewi turn left along another lane to go past a camp site and reach the toilets just inland of the beach at Cymdu, 21m from Cardigan.

From the beach at Cymdu climb back up onto the clifftop. After the first headland there is a fort called Castell Bach defended to landward by a ditch and rampart and then the path descends into a ravine. There is another stream to cross after another mile and then the path climbs back up to about 300ft and passes a recently reconditioned lookout shelter with a seat and information board. After another mile the path drops down into the northern edge of New Quay (Ceinewydd), 25m from Cardigan. The town has several shops and charming Georgian and Victorian houses from when it was an important port. Plans to make it the terminus of the Union of England and Ireland railway came to nothing and the last ship was built here in 1898. Big sheds at the end of Rock Terrace cover tanks for storing lobsters, most of which are exported to France. The church of St Llwchairn was rebuilt in 1863 but retains a Norman font and a carved beam over the west doorway, and there is a fine Congregational chapel (Capel Annibynol) of 1860 at the top end of the town.

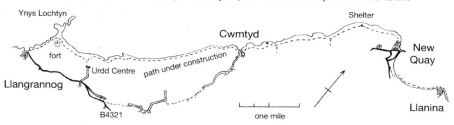

*The harbour at New Quay*

The junction of the A486 and B4342 lies on a headland between two bays just beyond the tourist office in Newquay. Follow B4342 past the lifeboat station and up to where it bends left at a T-junction. After another 300 yards fork left down Bronswen Lane, actually more of a track. Turn left at a T-junction and then go left down steps onto the beach for half a mile since beyond there is only a caravan site and no path as such. On reaching the River Lleithi (crossed by stepping stones) make a short detour inland on a woodland path along the west side of the river and then keep to the right to reach the small church of Llanina, dedicated to St Ina, a 7th century king of Wessex supposed to have been shipwrecked in this vicinity. The church was mostly rebuilt in the mid 19th century but retains an old font and a beam with an oak twig pattern from the former screen. At one time there was a thriving ship-building industry here. In the late 1930s Lord Howard de Waldon took up residence in the old mansion you will pass by before arriving at the church. He was friendly with Dylan Thomas, who used to write in a shed in the garden here during 1944. Here he wrote several poems and the first part of Under Milk Wood, although he was still working on it when he lived in Oxfordshire in 1947 and only completed it in America in 1953. Characters living in "Llareggub" (spell it backwards!) were based on people Dylan Thomas knew when living in New Quay during the war years. You will already have passed two sign boards with information about Dylan Thomas's activities in the town and the mansion here at Llanina bears one of the blue plaques set on local buildings associated with him.

After crossing the river stay on the edge of the shingle beach for another three quarters of a mile to reach a track climbing up from SN16599 (ie further east than it appears on the Landranger map), just past what looks like a ruined turret but isn't. At a crossing of tracks turn left. This crossing can be reached by an alternative route which takes you inland earlier up steps at a red marker, past some toilets, and go left when the lane bends right and take the path left just as you reach some buildings. The climb up from the crossing is on a good wide grassy track, one of the most pleasant sections of the whole walk. The path drops to cross a stream after a mile and isn't as good afterwards, although it is quite walkable for the remaining two and a half miles into Aberaeron, which is 30m from Cardigan.

*Llanina Church*

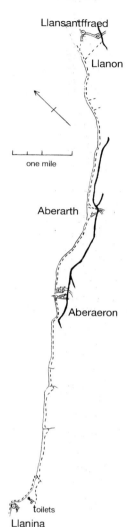

Llansantffraed
Llanon
one mile
Aberarth
Aberaeron
toilets
Llanina

ABERAERON is a planned town and port laid out after Susannah and Alban Thomas Jones of Ty-Glyn (by Afon Aeron 3m to to the SE) obtained Parliamentary sanction for piers and a harbour in 1807. There is an inner harbour with a sill across its entrance so that it retains enough water to float small vessels at low tide when the outer harbour is mostly reduced to mud banks. Names such as Regent St and Waterloo St indicate the date of construction, although Alban Square dates from 1850s and the gothic church is of 1875. Earlier are the Tabernacl and Peniel chapels of the 1830s, before which services were held in houses or warehouses.There was once a box-ferry suspended from a wire in which visitors were slowly cranked across the harbour mouth. The town was noted for shipbuilding, especially schooners, but declined after the railways took much of coastal trade of west Wales, the last ship being built in 1884. The well-house and the name Chalybeate Street are reminders of later ambitions for Aberaeron as a spa-town. There is a good range of shops and places to eat, drink and stay.

The next two mile section of coast path to Aberarth is fairly low lying and has recently been re-aligned following collapse of sections of the low cliffs carrying the original route. The tower visible high up on the right has a tunnel vault inside and may be 13th century. It stands at the west end of the church of St David (Llandewi Aberarth) half a mile SW of Aberarth, which offers no services to walkers. On the approach to the village take the track inland to cross Afon Arth on A487 and then use another track off left to the shore again. Keep right at the junction of paths before the climb up, although in fact the left path brings you back to the same place via a longer way round.

The last mile along the cliff edge from Morfa Mawr to the church of St Bridget at Llansantffraed of the three mile section from Aberarth is a new section of path, unmarked across the fields and only deliniated by the new signs, stiles and gates. St Bridget's is a 19th century church with box pews and a slate-hung south wall, but the substantial west tower is 15th century. The main settlement here is Llanon, 36m from Cardigan, straddling the A 487 a third of a mile to the SE, where there is a pub and shop, the last such services for the next eleven miles into Aberystwyth.

*The outer harbour at Aberaeron*

Follow the path past Llansantffraed church which leads out to cross several fields before re-joining the coast just before the Craiglas limekilns, which were once served by a jetty. A half mile section of new path then leads to where it is necessary to go inland along a lane. Just before joining A487 go left to cross Afon Wyre (unless you want to visit the pub or mostly 19th century church at Llanrhystud) and turn left along the road serving a camp site. The path actually climbs up alongside one edge of the camping field. At a division of paths go left and drop slightly to come out close to the shore. For the next five miles the path is relatively easy since there are no deep ravines to cross and navigation presents no great difficulties, with several new signposts.

It passes a boarded-up farmhouse at Pantyrallad, and another empty farm in a more derelic condition at Ffos-las. Beyond here the path climbs and heads inland to reach the farm track down to Cwm Ceirw. Turn right onto the track (away from the farm far below). Just after turning left at a T-junction a path drops steeply down to the left to cut a corner off. It is ill-defined but there are several marker posts to indicate the way. Cross over the track onto a path above the camp site at Morfa Bychan. The path climbs to 400ft before dropping down to a flat track which eventually runs between the shore and the Afon Ystwyth. About 300yards after crossing the river go left on A487 to cross the Afon Rheidol draining into the harbour to the soujth of the headland on which lies the original old part of the town of Aberystwyth, 47m from Cardigan. The town is by far the largest on the route and offers the best range of shops and services.

*Llansantffraed Church*

*Limekilns at Craiglas, near Llanon*

Two hundred years ago Aberystwyth was the fourth largest town in Wales and was then a busy port in which were based 2000 small vessels. Once a walled town, and still retaining its late 13th century layout, it declined as a port with the coming of the railways, but gained a new lease of life as a seaside resort and university town. The railway connections to Shrewsbury and Barmouth and Pwllheri remain open, and also the narrow guage Vale of Rheidol steam railway of 1902 up to Devil's Bridge, but the line down through Ceredigion into South Wales has long gone, so that it is necessary to go through Hereford and Shrewsbury to reach the town by rail from Cardiff. Aberystwyth has a Shrewsbury postcode too, to double the insult of such dependance upon services through England.

On Pendinas, the hill between the mouths of the Rheidol asnd Ystwyth, is a fine Iron Age fort and a monument of the Waterloo period. The de Clares built an earth and timber castle a mile to the south in 1110, near the original mouth of the Ystwyth. It was burned by the Welsh in 1136 and 1142. The castle of Aberheidol burned in 1164 by Rhys ap Gruffydd was either on that site or at Plas Crug to the east of the present town. The castle on the headland west of the town was one of several new castles begun after Edward I's defeat of Llewelyn ap Gruffydd in 1277. Originally called Llanbadarn after the settlement and large 13th century cruciform church of that name a mile and a half to the east, it has been known as Aberystwyth since the 15th century. It was a lozenge-shaped building with circular corner towers and inner and outer gatehouses in line facing the town, there being two concentric lines of defences. Because it could be supplied by sea from Bristol the castle was able with withstand a long siege during the Welsh revolt of 1294. In 1404 Owain Glyndwr was only able to take the castle after the supply ship was captured and he retained possession until it was recaptured by Prince Henry (later Henry V) in 1408. Thomas Bushell set up a mint in the castle in 1637, using silver and lead from local mines. The castle fell to Parlimentary forces in 1646 after a long siege and in 1649 was blown up and reduced to its present fragmentary state. The stone circle in the ruins (free access) was prepared for the Gorsedd ceremonies when a National Eisteddfod was held here in 1952.

*Part of the main inner gatehouse of Aberystwyth Castle*

*View of Aberystwyth from Constitution Hill*

NE of Aberystwyth castle lie St Michael's church of 1889-1907 with an earlier chancel of 1833, and the College, originally an hotel built in 1864 by Thomas Savin, but which soon afterwards became the centre of the University. The latter has now transferred to a new set of buildings of the 1930s onwards on Penglais Hill, a mile to the east, and in the middle of them lies the National Library of Wales (Llyfgell Genedlaethol Cymru), founded in 1907, one of six libraries entitled under the Copyright Act of 1911 to copies of every book published in this country. It has a fine collection of old prints, maps and Welsh language books and documents.

Beyond the College Victorian terraces extend round the shingle beach to the foot of Constitution Hill. Here is a selection of hotels and B&B places, although cheaper ones tend to be further inland. The tourist office lies just inland from the truncated pier of 1864 and at the far end is a cable-operated cliff railway of 1896.

*Cliff Railway up Constitution Hill, Aberystwyth*

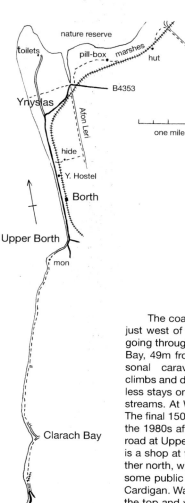

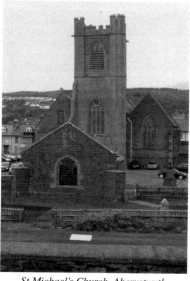

*St Michael's Church, Aberystwyth*

The coast path climbs up beside the cliff railway and passes just west of the summit of Constitution Hill. It then drops down, going through the end of a belt of dying conifers to reach Clarach Bay, 49m from Cardigan, a resort with both residential and seasonal caravans and a shop and bar. There are several steep climbs and descents over the next three miles as the path more or less stays on the cliff edge but has to cross the valleys of several streams. At Wallog, in one of the valleys, is yet another lime kiln. The final 150ft climb is over a hill bearing a war memorial rebuilt in the 1980s after destruction by a lightning strike. The path joins a road at Upper Borth and this leads to B4353 heading north. There is a shop at the road junction, and several others, plus pubs, further north, with a useful grouping of a foodshop, tourist office and some public toilets just south of Borth railway station, 54m from Cardigan. Walking across the beach is difficult since it is shingle at the top and wet sand divided by wooden groins lower down, but there is a walkway between the beach and the main road except for the first 300 yards or so. The largest of the hotels at Borth was taken over for a year in 1876 by the Uppingham School, which came here after a fatal typhoid epidemic in its own premises. Ancient tree stumps revealed at low tides support the legend of the submerged land of Cantref y Gwaelod.

Beyond the station the road passes the youth hostel. Further north the road has neither a pavement or public verge and a golf course occupies the land between it and the shingle top of the beach. However, not far north of the hostel a path crosses the railway on a level crossing and goes past a bird hide forming an open shelter on the way out to meet the path along the embankment along the west bank of Afon Leri. Signs proclaim this area as a nature reserve and tell you about the birds to be seen. East of here is the huge bog of Cors Fochno, noted for rare plants. Head north and cross the river after a mile on a footbridge beside the railway, which is then re-crossed on another level crossing. For access to the dunes at the mouth of the Dovey, 58m from Cardigan, turn left to recross Afon Leri, turn right on a path for half a mile to Ynyslas and then go right, heading north to where there are toilets at the carpark at the road end.

*The beach at Borth*

This final section is not strictly part of the Ceredigion coast path but provides a varied and attractive walk from Ynyslas to join up with the Owain Glyndwr Way at Machynlleth. On reaching B4353 after crossing Afon Leri and the railway turn right a very short distance to pick up a path on the left leading north out to the embankment separating the agricultural land from the marshland of the estuary. The map shows no path along the embankment but there is one of sorts, since this is part of the nature reserve, with more signboards about the fauna and flora. It passes a wartime pillbox just before a pair of bridges over the wet ditch south of the embankment. The railway occupies the embankment for the next half a mile, so it is necessary to walk on the salt marshes, which is feasible, although a little damp underfoot in places and several water-channels have to be jumped over. Be careful if it is close to being high tide, when the ground will be even wetter. Just beyond the plate-layers' hut on the other side of the railway the embankment divides again from the railway and although lower than previously it provides a drier route round to where a path running along the embankment on the SW side of Afon Cletwr runs under the railway bridge. Access onto the north end of this path from beside another nature reserve signboard involves a tricky and potentially muddy crossing of a tidal stream and at high tide the path under the bridge, which is 59m from Cardigan, is submerged. Take care.

Follow the path on the embankment for over a mile to reach B4353 and turn left down it to A487 at Tre'r-dol, where there is a petrol-station shop. Go left down the main road for 200 yards to find a path forking off up through woodland on the right. It climbs 160ft to give a view of the estuary. Cross over a lane and go through a field, looking right to find a bridge. The path bends left to follow the stream downhill before climbing a bit and meeting a track on which turn left down to A487. Turn right for half a mile along the main road to where a path is signed off to the right. After a short double-hedged section go left over a bridge and climb up in woodland behind houses. Join a track and go right when it immediately divides. At a right hand bend take the path going straight on to meet a road. Go left down it and at a junction take the path almost opposite gradually descending to a footbridge over Afon Einion. Turn left after crossing, to come below a house and turn left onto its access track for 250 yards until a path goes off to the right. This path is good and clear, marked by posts, and offers fine views of the upper reaches of the Dovey Estuary.

*Machynlleth from Owain Glyndwr's Way*

*Junction of route with Owain Glyndwr's Way, near Machynlleth*

Descend to a road opposite a farm and turn right, climbing quite steeply for two thirds of a mile to find a path up through woods, although an open gate beforehand allows a very steep short cut up to a gate. Beyond the path is faint as it crosses a saddle but is clearer as it descends beside a wall. Keep left, by the wall, when it divides, and drop down to turn left on a road by a house. Go 300yards along the road to find another lane going sharply back to the right. Turn right after crossing Afon Llynant, which marks the boundary between Ceredigion and Powys. Beyond a house the track enters a forest and climbs for over a mile. Ignore a couple of tracks descending to the right. At a clearing the track passes through a sequence of gates to reach a house but you can cut the corner off by turning left after the first gate onto a footpath. Go over a crossing of paths and at another division drop down to to right to meet the access road of the house. Follow it to the bend of another road and go left (effectively straight on). After the road bends left turn sharply back right on another road down as far as where a gate on the left marks a path going steeply up through a field to another clearly visible gate. Turn left onto another road, still climbing. After 400 yards Owain Glyndwr's Way comes in from the right on a track. Remain on the road until the way shortly leaves it on a path to the right. It descends on a track which has the so-called Roman Steps (actually cut in the 1870s). On reaching the main road the way avoids following it into the middle of Machynlleth, and goes instead through the park of the mansion of Plas Machynlleth, round to issue through ornamental gates onto A489 opposite where the Parliament House is, 71 miles from Cardigan.

With a population of about 2500 Machynlleth is not a large place and the range of shops here is not particularly impressive, but it has always been of importance, and once had no fewer than 24 inns, the old bridge carrying A487 over the Dovey being the lower crossing point of that river. This road, called Doll St from a Toll House on one side of it, passes the railway station and before that the church St Peter with a 15th century west tower remodelled in the 18th century and a main body of 1827 replacing the cruciform 13th century building. The font under the tower is also 15th century. In 1404 Owain Glyndwr was proclaimed Prince of Wales by his supporters at Machynlleth and part of his much altered and restored Parliament house still remains. Nearby is the tourist office, and there are several interesting old town houses here in Maen Gwyn St, which is named after an old signpost stone set into a house wall. There was once another toll house on this street. Side steets with the names of Garrison (Gariswn) and Barracks recall when Parliamentary forces had to be kept here to maintain the peace after the second Civil War of 1649, following King Charles I's execution. At the junction of the three main road is a clock tower of 1873 built by the Marquess of Londonderry, whose family had inherited Plas Mychynlleth from the Edwardes family. Now owned by the town council, the house has 19th century facades grafted onto a 16th and 17th century core and houses an exhibition. Near the clock tower is a medieval house called Royal House, having been supposedly visited either by Henry Tudor on his way to victory at Bosworth or the less fortunate Charles I.

# FURTHER READING

The Old Parish Churches of Mid Wales, Mike Salter, 2nd edition 2003 (see list opposite)
The Old Parish Churches of South-West Wales, Mike Salter, 1994 (see list opposite)
The Castles of South-West Wales, Mike Salter, 1996 (see list opposite)
Companion Guide to South Wales, Peter Howel & Elizabeth Beazley, 1977
The Shell Guide to Wales, Wynford Vaughan-Thomas and Alun Llewellyn, 1969
The Medieval Towns of Wales, Ian Soulsby, 1983

## USEFUL WEBSITES AND OTHER INFORMATION

www.backpackersclub.co.uk - Club for those interested in backpacking in the UK.
www.campingandcaravanningclub.co.uk - Join to obtain details of extra camp sites.
www.geocaching.com          - Finding caches using a Global Positioning System
www.ldwa.org.uk             - The Long Distance Walkers Association.
www.IndependentHostelGuide - Guide to independent hostels, new edition each year.
www.nationaltrail.co.uk      - Details of long-distance trails in UK.
www.traveline.org.uk         - Travel information throughout the UK
www.yha.org.uk              - The Youth Hostels Association of England and Wales.
National Rail Enquiries:   08457 48 49 50.   For buses ring Traveline:  0870 608 2 608
Tourist Offices:  Cardigan, New Quay, Aberaeron, Aberystwyth, Borth, Machynlleth.
Youth Hostels:  Borth (on route), Poppit Sands (four miles west of start at Cardigan).
    Corris  (five miles north of finish of walk at Machynlleth)
    All Youth Hostels in Britain are open to non-members - at a small additional price.
Maps can be obtained through the Backpackers Club at a substantially reduced price.
The Backpackers Club provides members with info on farm and wild camping places.
Members of the Backpackers Club and the Long Distance Walkers Association obtain
    discounts on equipment from certain shops.  Enquire for details.
The National Trust owns three estates traversed by the coast path: Mwnt, Penbryn and
    Mynachdy'r Graig. From Aberaeron it is possible to walk down an old railway track
    for two and a half miles to the estate of Llanerchaeron, with a working organic farm
    and a villa designed in the 1790s by John Nash for the Pnonsonby Lewes family.

*Tresaith*